Blue Eyes
Wide Open

RACHEL SPIGELMAN

This is a story based
on my husband Mark's
early childhood.

I dedicate this book to Mark
and his heroic mama and papa,
Gutcha and Majloch.

And to the memory of the
one and half million Jewish children
who did not survive the Holocaust.

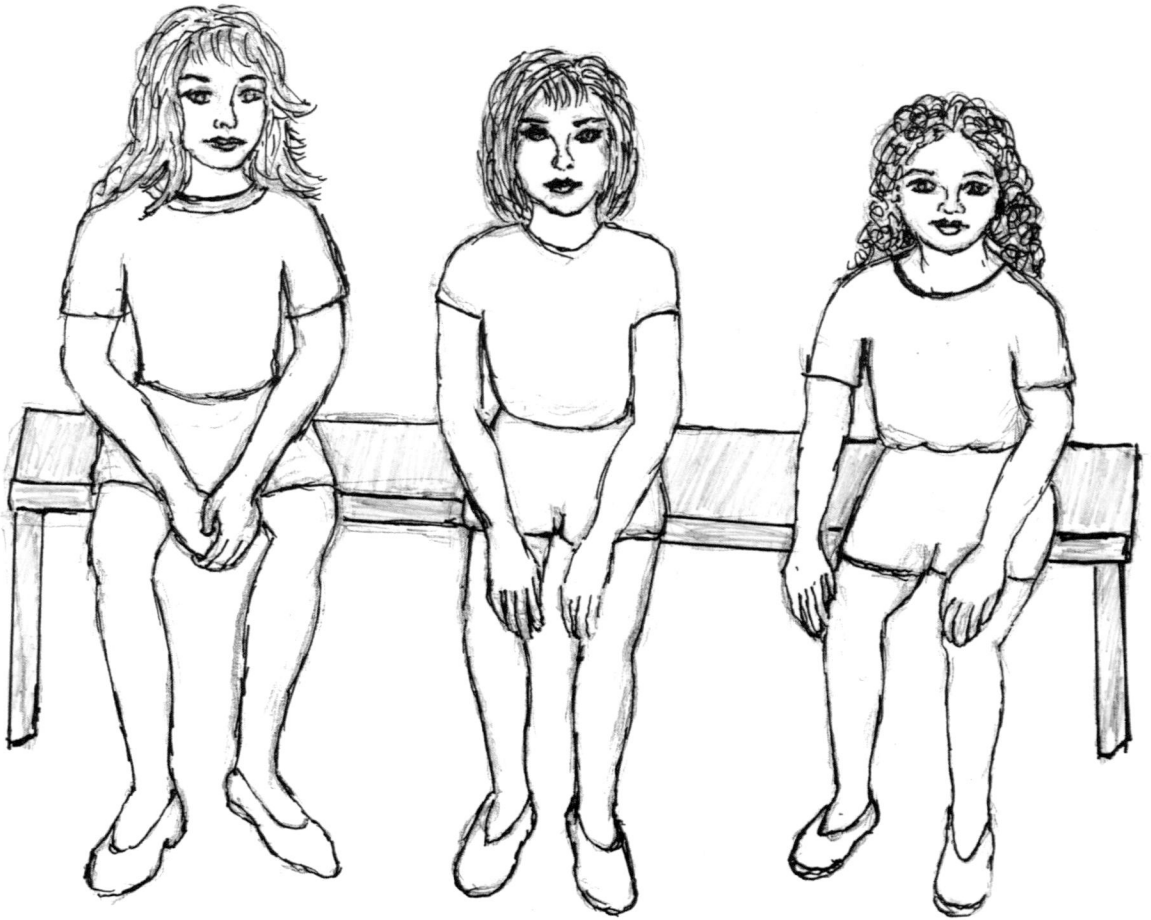

It's Time to Tell

There they were, my three beloved granddaughters, sitting in front of me, big shining eyes full of anticipation as they waited to hear my childhood story.

After returning from school, they had hugged me and, in unison, said,

"Grandpa, today is Holocaust Memorial Day. We know it's a sad day for you."

Effie, the eldest, then said, "We believe we are old enough now to understand what happened to you. It's time you told us everything you remember, so it will never, ever be forgotten!"

I looked at them lovingly, as a grandfather does. Although they were young and wide-eyed with wonder, they were ready to hear the story of our family's survival in the face of unbearable suffering.

"Alright, my darlings. I agree, it's time. As you know, I was a very small child in Poland during that traumatic time of the Second World War. My memory is of separate events, in no particular order."

Seeing my hesitation, Nella,
the youngest, urged me to
continue. "Please start with
the first story you remember."

The German Officer

I closed my eyes and the words tumbled out.
I saw myself and my mama on a small street
leading to a square. She told me that we were
going to the bread shop. Suddenly, I could hear
dogs barking, people screaming, and pounding
boots coming closer and closer.

Mama picked me up and tried to turn away,
but it was too late. Two uniformed men grabbed
us and pushed us towards the square.

Ahead of us, I could see sad and scared-looking
people in two groups surrounded by the
Polish police. German officers looked on with
expressionless faces.

We were pushed to the line on the left. There
were old people there, and women and children
like us.

Mama turned, and still carrying me in her arms, started moving quickly to the line on the right, where the young people were standing. A policeman noticed us and struck her with his baton while ordering her to return to the line on the left. As soon as the policeman turned away, Mama started walking to the right again. The policeman came running after us. This time he hit us with his baton, as hard as he could, as he pushed us back to the left line.

Mama's face turned white and I started crying.

"Shush," said Mama. "Just smile and open your blue eyes, my little girl."

Then she started moving us to the right again.

As the policeman grabbed Mama's arm once more, a German officer came over and ordered him to let us go. He looked into my eyes and, with a gentle voice, said, "Little one, you remind me so much of my little girl who I have not seen in a long time. I miss her every day. Madam, look after your daughter and go home."

Mama put me down and, as we walked away hand-in-hand, I looked up at her and asked about the children in the square. "Where are those bad policemen taking them?"

With tears in her eyes, she replied, "I don't know."

As we kept walking, I felt an urge to pee, but I knew that I was not allowed to pull my underpants down in public, so when we arrived home I was a little wet!

As I opened my eyes and looked over at my granddaughters, I saw Gilli, the second eldest, wipe away her tears. "That was a close escape, Grandpa," she said. "Please tell us more."

On the Tram

I nodded and continued telling my story.

Mama used to take me out every now and again, but Papa always stayed at home. I did not understand why. As a matter of fact, I did not understand many things, but I felt that it was important to do whatever I was told.

When we were out, I was told to open my blue eyes, to smile, and never to cry. I was not allowed to talk when there were people around and Mama always spoke German, not Polish, which was our language at home.

On one outing, I fell asleep while on the tram with Mama and woke up feeling frightened, only to realise my head was resting on the black sleeve of a German officer sitting next to me. Even though I liked being on the tram, I did not like sitting next to German officers.

The front carriages were reserved for Germans and the Poles were only allowed in the back carriages. Mama had chosen to sit in the front carriage because we had no identification papers. She felt it was the safest way to travel without being asked to show proof that she was not a Jew.

A woman boarded at one of the stops and, as she passed our row, she stopped, pointed to Mama and in Polish shouted, "I know her, she is a Jew!" Mama immediately looked at the German officer and said, in her best German,

"Are you going to let this woman insult me?"

The officer stood up, grabbed the woman and pushed her out of the tram, then came back to our seats and apologised to Mama.

We got off a few stops later and went home without getting any shopping done.

Upon our return, Papa took one look at Mama and gathered her up in his arms. She was pale and trembling all over.

As sad and as shaken as I felt, I also knew that we were not going to have anything to eat that night. And I was already hungry.

My granddaughters were quiet for a while. Then Effie said, "Our great-grandma was such a courageous woman, I would have loved to have met her."

"Me too!" agreed the others.

Nella then asked me,

"Remind us why you were dressed up as a girl?"

"As you know," I answered, "the Jewish faith requires that all baby boys be circumcised. So when the Germans were hunting for Jews, the first thing they would do was pull down little boys' pants to discover if they were Jewish. That is why I spent most of the war years dressed as a girl."

The Shooter

"My next memory, girls, is the most painful for me
because I found myself all alone without my mama
and papa."

I was in a room just below a roof that I later learned
was an attic. Some heat and light came through an
opening in the corner. I could hear voices speaking
in Polish—mostly angry voices. I had no idea how
long I was there for.

Gilli asked me,

"Were you ever told why
you were in that attic
and separated from your
mama and papa?"

"Yes," I answered, "the raids were getting
more frequent, and many more children were
disappearing. So they gave some money to
our Polish neighbours who agreed to hide me."

My next memory is of being hidden in a sack and carried on my papa's back. All of a sudden, I heard gunshots and a voice screaming in German, "Halt!" Papa froze on the spot and I started to tremble. I was pulled out of the sack by a huge German officer who threw me down, making me land with a thud.

He pointed his pistol at my head and shouted at Papa, "You know that children are not allowed in the camp."

Papa replied in a shaking voice, "If you kill my child, you will have to kill me too."

The officer hesitated for a minute and, to Papa's surprise, said, "I will let you go for now because you are brave—if somewhat stupid—but if I see this child again, I will shoot you both!"

Papa then took me into the camp where I was reunited with Mama.

This officer was known all over the camp as 'The Shooter' because when he encountered anyone he did not like, he would often shoot them. We got very lucky that night.

I looked at the girls' sad faces and asked them, "Do you want me to stop now?"

They shook their heads and Nella said,

"Please continue, we want to learn about everything you went through. You are very special to us."

Gilli spoke up, "What puzzles me is how your papa was able to get out of the camp, then collect you and bring you back with him?"

"This is hard to answer," I told her. "It was only much later in life that I heard bits and pieces about what happened to us. Mama and Papa did not like to discuss those events with me much, I think because they wanted to spare my feelings."

Little did my granddaughters know I was still having nightmares about the events I did remember.

"So," asked Effie, "who did tell you?"

"Some of my parents' friends, who always talked about the war time. And, believe it or not, as soon as I married your grandma, Mama and Papa started telling her our story."

The Kombinator
(The Trickster)

The camp was a group of workshops that supplied many of the German army's needs. Papa was in charge of the shoe repair shop and Mama helped him. This way they were able to stay in the camp and were not sent away.

From time to time at the start of their captivity, Papa was able to leave the camp to get the materials he needed for repairing shoes. It must have been during one of these trips that he was able to collect me from the attic.

I don't know how long we continued to exist under those conditions. I knew that I had uncles and cousins nearby who worked in other workshops, but I was not let out of our room, and I rarely saw anyone.

One day, I heard my parents whispering and
I crawled under the table so I could hear them.
They were talking about my papa's younger brother,
Chayim who was known as 'the kombinator'.

"That sounds like a tricky word," said Gilli.

I did not know what it meant at the time. All I knew
was that Chayim used to drop in to give us some
extra food and occasionally a piece of chocolate
for me.

"So, what does that word mean and what were they
whispering about?" asked Effie.

"Being a 'kombinator' meant that he was able to help
his family by tricking the German guards, especial-
ly the officer known as 'The Shooter', by playing
a card game called poker, and keeping the officer
amused by losing money to him."

Mama and Papa's whispering sounded very scary.
My uncle Chayim had told them that more and
more people were disappearing from the camp and
the ghetto, and that it was becoming harder to find
food. Mama started to cry and I wanted to hug her,
but I didn't want them to know I was hiding under
the table.

Later, I heard Papa tell her that he and Uncle
Chayim had decided to dig a bunker big enough to
hide some of our family from the German officers.

Papa got busy in the room where he repaired boots
and shoes. He separated the shelves, broke the
walls, and dug out a hole which ended up being
quite big.

"That must have been such hard work," said Nella.

"Yes, it was," I answered. "He was desperate to save us."

The Bunker

The next thing I remember was being alone in
the bunker.

In one of my nightmares, I am sitting in the dark.
There is a thick smell of old leather shoes, and the
harsh sound of German voices barking orders for
Papa to repair the boots faster. *"Schnell! Schnell!"*
they shout over and over. I can't make a sound,
or I might be discovered.

"When do you have these dreams?" asked Effie.
"They must be terrifying!"

I have had these nightmares as far back as I can
remember. I still do. And Effie was right, they are
terrifying. Even though it all happened a long time
ago, as I told my granddaughters my story, I felt
frightened all over again.

I was smuggled into the bunker through the shoe repair room and was told to sit there quietly and to sleep as much as I could. Mama brought me food and sometimes sat with me and told me funny stories. But most of the time, I was alone.

Very little light came through the wall, just like in the attic before, but I felt better in the bunker because at least I knew that Mama and Papa were nearby.

"Did you have anything to play with?" asked Nella.

I couldn't recall having any toys, but I did have
a little friend that was either a mouse or a rat;
I didn't know if it was the same creature that came
through the small hole each time. It would visit
when I had some food, mostly bread that I shared
with it, and while it nibbled, I would touch it and
feel its warmth. It made me feel as though I was
not completely alone.

"Are you ok, Grandpa?" asked Effie. "It must be making you feel sad to bring up all these memories."

"You are right, but I am also glad to share my memories with you, my dear granddaughters, because it is important that you tell our family's story to your children and grandchildren one day, so the events of that terrible time are not forgotten and will never happen again."

In unison, all three girls said, "Amen." Their encouragement reassured me that it was the right time for them to hear these stories.

After what seemed like a long time with just Mama and Papa, Uncle Chayim, my cousin Manny and a few more relatives hid with us. They were quiet and looked scared and sad.

After a day and a night, Papa and Chayim left, but quickly returned to tell us it was time to leave. Mama held my hand tightly and took me outside into the light of day that I had not seen in a very long time.

The Garbage Dump

We walked cautiously out of the bunker to find that the camp was empty. All the German guards were gone, and the gates were open. Everyone went in different directions to look for new places to hide. Mama, Papa and I ended up at the town's garbage dump. Even though it was smelly, it was warm and it felt safe.

The girls looked upset so I paused the story for a moment. Knowing the next part would be difficult to hear, I tried to reassure them.

"Don't look sad, my darlings. After all, I survived and I'm here now, telling you my story."

One day, Mama left to search for food but, many hours later, she had not returned. It grew dark and I was hungry. I could see that Papa looked worried and I suddenly felt afraid. "Where is she?" I asked him. Papa took me by the hand and we left the garbage dump.

After walking for a while, we stopped at some railroad tracks. I looked up at Papa and saw the pain in his face. I asked him why we were stopping there. He said we were going to lie down on the tracks and that it would soon be over.

I knew that meant the train would run us over and that we would die. I grew angry and cried out, "You can lie on the tracks, but I will not. I want to live!" After a few moments, Papa realised that I was not prepared to give up. With tears in his eyes, he took my hand and we walked back to the garbage dump. When we arrived, Mama was there with a basket of food.

The girls looked at me with wonder and Gilli said, "You were so brave! What happened after that?"

The Farmhouse

When she was in town looking for food, Mama, by chance, had run into a cousin of Papa's. He told her about a woman who owned a farmhouse near a big German camp. She was willing to shelter a Jewish family and hide them from the German guards provided they could pay her. Luckily, we could.

While living at the farmhouse there were times when we could hear loud voices speaking in German coming from downstairs and we had to hide in a wardrobe. I remember one time I begged my parents to please let me go to the bathroom, but they held on to my hands and put a finger to their lips to shush me.

We could not make a sound
until the Germans went away,
or we may have been caught.
We had to hide in the wardrobe
like this on many nights, but
luckily no-one ever came upstairs.

Papa told me that the German guards would come to the house to sit by the fire because it was cold, so cold and windy that sometimes it sounded like someone was knocking on the window. Mama told me the cold meant it was nearly Christmas time.

The food at the farmhouse was the same each day: potato, cabbage, soup, bread, sometimes an apple to share, and plain tea to drink. The woman hiding us must have heard Mama mention Christmas, because the next day there was an extra plate on the tray with a slice of bread spread with white cheese and sugar sprinkled on it, as well as two paper-wrapped lollies, one grey and one blue.

"This is for the child," she said. "It is Christmas day tomorrow!"

Even today, I think that was the best meal I have ever had.

The War is Over

"It is hard to believe everything that happened to you, but I understand it now," said Effie. Gilli and Nella nodded their heads in agreement.

"Yes," I replied, "I also find it hard to believe all that happened to us and to so many other families during those years."

We sat in silence to reflect for a while, but there was another story I wanted to tell them. A story of hope.

At the bedroom in the farmhouse, the one window was covered with a dark curtain. I was warned never to touch it and certainly not to peek through it. One morning, I woke up before Mama and Papa to the sound of loud booms. I couldn't stop myself from lifting the curtain to peek outside.

The first thing I noticed was the white field covered with snow. My eyes started hurting as I was blinded by the light after not looking outside for such a long time.

After a few minutes my eyes got used to the light and I could see men dressed in white crawling through the snow, pushing guns in front of them. They didn't look like German guns. I ran to Mama and Papa's bed, shook them till they woke up and pointed to the window. I couldn't talk because I was trembling with excitement.

They looked out the window to see the Russian soldiers who, on that day, defeated the Germans and liberated the nearby camp. Mama started crying and Papa hugged her as they yelled,

"The war is over! The war is over!"

"What did you do when they said the war was over? You must have felt so happy," said Gilli.

I felt I had to do something, so I took off my nightgown and ran to the door. Mama put her hand out to stop me and asked what I was doing. I told her that because the war was over, I wanted to go outside to pee in public! She told me that it was not such a good idea in the freezing cold, and with a smile I had not seen in a very long time she said, "It would be best that you wait for the summer to do that!"

After the War

Although the war had ended, it did not mean that everything returned to normal. I felt as proud and free as a little child who had never experienced freedom could feel. And I could be a boy for all to see; my hair was cut short, and I wore trousers and shirts.

We moved into a large house close to the town I was born in. Papa posted notices with our name and address all over, so that any relatives who had survived the war could find us and stay with us if they needed shelter and help. I remember that quite a few people came by.

Some months later, after the summer, I was sent to school. I was the only Jewish boy there and on the first day some children started shoving me around in the playground, calling me a Jew and blaming me for starting the war and killing Jesus. I told them I was not alive when the war started and that I didn't know who Jesus was, but they kept shoving me. Some even hit me.

"Were there any teachers in the playground to stop them?" asked Effie.

"Some teachers passed by, but they didn't pay any attention to my troubles, and when Mama and Papa picked me up that day, they decided not to send me to that school again."

"So, after that did you stay at home all the time?" asked Nella.

"Sometime later, after more survivors came to town, a small Jewish school opened, and I was sent there."

"Did you have friends at that school?" asked Gilli.

"Not that I remember."

I had never played with children
before then, only mice. I did not
know how to make friends, and
neither did the other children.
Like me, they started their life
in captivity, living in silence,
often hungry, mostly alone, and
always scared.

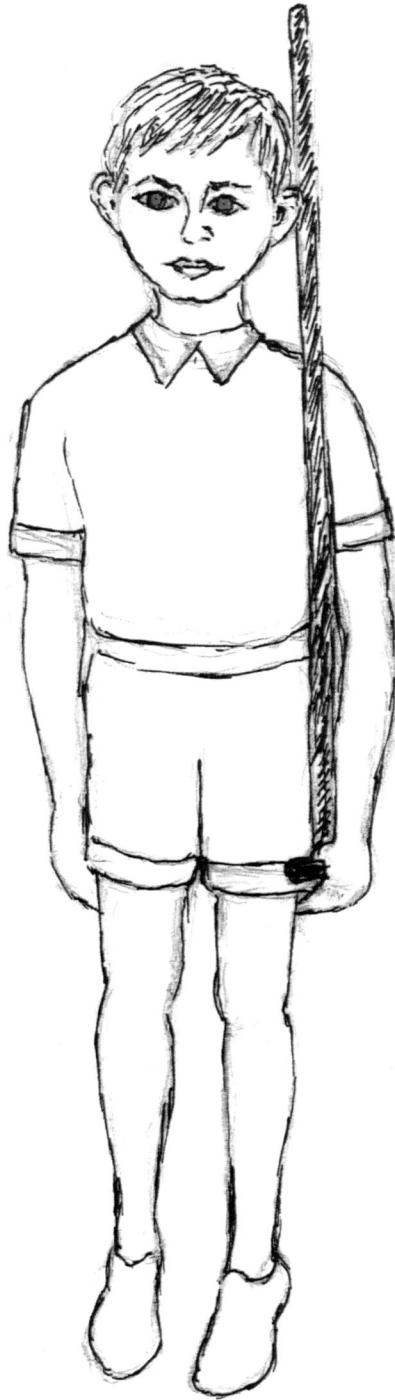

A Final Visit

"There is one last story I would like to share with you. Before leaving Poland to move to Australia, we visited the largest camp where many of our family as well as many others died at the hands of the Germans."

Even though it was a sunny day when we arrived at the camp, to me it looked grey and deserted. There were other people walking around who, like Mama and Papa, looked very sad. We entered buildings that Mama told me had held innocent Jewish prisoners before they had been led to their deaths. I grew angry. I took my papa's walking stick from him and waved it defiantly as I marched towards a guard's hut, shouting at the top of my lungs,

"I never want to be a prisoner. I want to protect people, not hurt them."

We are Survivors

Tears brimmed in my eyes as the girls rushed over to hug and kiss me, and I felt that it was the best day of my life. They were tears of joy for those of us who survived, but also tears of sadness for those of us who did not.

Mama and Papa decided we needed to move as far away from Poland as possible, which is why they chose Australia, a country where we could live freely and start a wonderful new life.

As I finished my story, I looked at my granddaughters once more. In that moment, I realised that they were also survivors.

I hoped they would pass my stories down through future generations to ensure that such terrible times never happened again—anywhere, to anyone.

Published by Real Publishing
www.realpublishing.com.au

Written and Illustrated by Rachel Spigelman
Edited by Georgie Raik-Allen and Romy Moshinsky
Designed by Marianna Berek-Lewis

With thanks to Ron Spigelman for his early
editorial assistance.

ISBN: 978-0-6456811-7-8

NATIONAL
LIBRARY
OF AUSTRALIA

A catalogue record for this
book is available from the
National Library of Australia

REAL
PUBLISHING